Keep making
lemonade!
Judy Endow

D1070322

making lemonade

HINTS FOR AUTISM'S HELPERS

JUDY ENDOW

ILLUSTRATIONS BY BEN AVERILL

Cambridge Book Review Press
2006

Cambridge Book Review Press
310 North Street
Cambridge, Wisconsin 53523
Editor: Bob Wake

Book and cover design by Nancy Zucker

ISBN-13: 978-0-9660376-5-4
ISBN-10: 0-9660376-5-0

Library of Congress Control Number: 2006921536

Printed in Canada

Order copies of this book online at the *Making Lemonade Store*
www.makinglemonadestore.com

This book is dedicated to:

my parents:
Del and Ruth Linders
who provided others during my growing up years who tried to figure "IT" out

my children:
David, Paul and Daniel
who provided three literal, concrete, daily reasons for me to get "IT" figured out

my kiddos:
Francis, LeVanba, Christos and all the rest
who have been and now are in my life,
for graciously allowing me to walk with them so we might all continue to figure "IT" out

and most of all

to my best friend:
Kate
who loves ME with or without having "IT" figured out

FOREWORD

I thought I knew.

I thought I did too.

We've been studying and working for years.

And now … I feel like a beginner.

Yes, a beginner with a teacher who is the clearest I've ever had.

Do you remember how we first connected with her?

Through words …

She read our words.

And said the colors matched.

I was so confused by that … at first.

Until we read her words.

Yes.

Remember? We felt the match, but still didn't understand the colors.

Then there were the e-mails! More words for all of us …

Words that made pictures for her and revealed to her more of our colors.

Then her words again … they made our "eyes leak," as she would say.

Her words touched our hearts.

Yes.

And remember? She was worried about that. How can words "touch" hearts, she asked.

She had touched ours … After all these years of study, all the kiddos we've seen and taught, workshops taken and given …

In our connection with her, we became new learners. Learning about things we thought we knew.

Learning about her, and what her life has been like …

If life gives you lemons, make lemonade. If life gives you autism—

—make poetry, the sweetest, most potent lemonade in the universe.

Through her book, Judy gently invites us to partake. Fill your glasses.

Drink deeply.

Cheers!

Kate McGinnity and Nan Negri are autism consultants and the authors of *Walk Awhile in My Autism: A manual of sensitivity presentations to promote understanding of people on the autism spectrum*, published in 2005 by Cambridge Book Review Press.

INTRODUCTION

Dear Teachers (and other helpers of people with autism),

Hello. I am Autism. I am Judy. I am a unique person just like you. Most of the time I like myself. A lot of the time I get frustrated. The things that cause me to become frustrated every day involve the Stuck of Autism. I can get stuck in so many ways I consider myself an expert on the topic! This is a good example of the saying, "When life gives you lemons, make lemonade." Each everyday little Stuck is like another lemon. Now, there are lots of things you can do with one lemon, but if you have lots of lemons then what? The way I see it is that you can:

1. throw them out,
2. let them rot and then throw them out,
   OR
3. make lemonade

I am an old lady (according to my son). All my life I've had lots of lemons. This means I have had lots of opportunities to try all three of these what-to-do-with-lots-of-lemons strategies. The corresponding end results of the above three strategies are:

1. immediate death,
2. slow death,
   OR
3. lemonade

It doesn't take a rocket scientist to figure it out. Of course we would all pick lemonade over death at any speed, immediate or slow!

The really great thing about this is that people with autism tend to have a lot of lemons. They often get stuck. So, if you are any kind of helper to a person on the autism spectrum you are indeed blessed. You are already on the road to success! You have an abundant, never-ending supply of lemons at your disposal. And no matter what, you do need lemons to make lemonade. This is a very profound truth. It can't be said enough:

You need lemons to make lemonade.

This means that if God (or your Principal or your Special Ed. Director) put lemons in your fruit basket, don't be trying to change them into oranges or apples or anything else. Even if you can rationalize that it is in the best interest of the lemons to become oranges so they might better fit in please don't go there. You will only use a lot of time, energy and days of the school year trying to change lemons into something they cannot ever become.

And, while you are busy trying to change lemons into oranges so they might better fit in, all of the fruit in your basket intuitively learns:

1. there is a BIG difference between Joey's lemons and our oranges,
2. oranges are best,
   AND
3. lemons are bad

You will never need to say these things or, indeed, even to think them. But if you are trying to change lemons into oranges this is what you will be teaching. And no matter how hard you try you cannot change the lemons of autism into oranges or into anything else neuro-typical. The best you can do is to help the lemons you see to become the best looking, best functioning lemons possible.

I think of my lemons of autism as the fruit of who I am. I was born wired to fit (or not to fit, depending upon your perspective) into this world. I cannot change my internal wiring any more than I can change my genes. I cannot change my lemons any more than I can change my blue eye color or my attached earlobes.

I have autism.
I have lemons.
I choose to learn how to make lemonade.

Will you help me learn how?

Sincerely,
The Stuck of Autism

MY SENSORY LEMONS

LEMONS OF IMPORTANCE

… because

they readily impact

    all of

        WHO she is

          HOW she is

            and her perception of

              her own life experience

             and

            everything in

          and of

        and about

      the world all around her

        the world outside of her being

          on the outside side

           of her skin

HEARING INTENTLY

Always too sensitive
    usually annoying
        overly fine-tuned
            is her hearing

    making
        ordinary human events of the day
          like watching TV
            too domineering.

The difference
    in loudness
        from show
          to commercial

    is so distracting
        most days
          TV's not
            worth it!

In bed
    her ears
        on the pillows
          must be just right

    so her heartbeats'
        loud whooshing
          won't keep her awake
            all night.

Sometimes
    this way
        of hearing
          comes in quite handy

    like when
        strange sounding car noises
        send her preventatively
          to the mechanic!

One night
        on the kitchen counter
                she heard
                        a pill drop.

    She
            got out of bed
                    and an overdose
                            stopped!

It's sometimes
        handy
            and sometimes
                    a struggle

    when hearing
            all
                    small sounds
                            is a daily normal.

EVERYDAY SOUNDS

Everyday sounds that

   jar the hairs
   or

   hurt the skin

   inside
   her ears:

   cellophane wrappers (like the kind on microwave popcorn)
   fake pianos (electronic keyboards)
   bicycle chains when peddling too fast
   bowling alley pins being knocked down
   pep band playing in the gym
   car tires traveling over wet highways
   diaper wipes being pulled out of the canister too fast

   hair blow-dryers
   markers squeaking on paper
   electric razors
   car heater fans on high
   grandma's ankle bones clicking and cracking (when she jiggles her foot)
   electric can-openers
   indoor swimming pool noise

   public bathrooms: toilets flushing and hand dryers whining
   clinking silverware in a cafeteria
   notebook paper being ripped out too fast
   two different ticking speeds of clocks in the same house
   the snapping of gum as it's being chewed
   lawn mowers

   weed whackers
   leaf blowers
   ice cubes banging against a glass glass
   a gerbil's exercise wheel (when the gerbil is in it)
   bird noises (some call it singing) inside a building
   clickety-clacking of the insides of a computer
   pairs of different sounding shoes walking on hard floors at the same time

WARRING COLORS

Colors are something her eyes   can readily see
        and when colors   match

            they tend to   give back
        a comfort   to   her eyes.

But when colors   don't match
        she can get   distracted

            and sometimes finds it harder to function
        when her attention needs to   be given

            over   to inside-her-skin   physical senses.

If world-people could see
        what happens   inside   to her body

            when colors are   clashing outside of her skin
        in the world   all around her

            this is what   they'd observe:

                Her eyes start   hurting
                    as if they are   burning.

                Sometimes tears   form
                and   leak   onto her face.

        Her insides become   dis   jointed

                with inside-her-skin
                molecules of

                her very   being
                trying to   m   o   v   e

        away from   each   other

                like sisters   and brothers
                in a family   feud—

                    kin   not getting along,
                    choosing up sides

and warring
with one another.

This causes a physical
aching inside.

Her muscles   get sore
and tired.

Over the years she has   learned
that for her   it's not a very wise choice

to remain   a long time
inside of a room

where the colors don't   match together.

WHAT STINKS AND WHAT DOESN'T

Sometimes people think the air   smells bad.

They notice it, maybe   make a comment,
    but then soon   forget it

    as their attention focuses
        back to whatever   their previous business

of the day   happened to be
    before they noticed   the odor.

For her   bad smells   are a bit more   intrusive

She notices them   quicker   than others
    and sometimes can   smell

    what nobody   else
        ever seems to   notice.

When the stench is   bad

    in the atmosphere
        on the   outside of her skin

    It   takes her   attention
        until she   can discover

    a way   to cope   with the stink
        or else   somehow   end it.

But she's become   smart   about stink.

She now   stops   to think
    and to   remind herself quite often

    that nobody   else
        will want   to know

    what stinks   to her
        and what   doesn't!

FOOD NAMES

A long time ago
        when Eve looked at the fruit

        and called it an apple
                (if this is what really happened)

        she must have been thinking of
        how that fruit looked

                and then, from that day on

                        every fruit that looked the same
                        was called "apple" by name

                        even though
                        after hundreds are eaten

                        no two have ever
                                tasted the same!

Hasn't anyone noticed that food
        called by a name

                never tastes the same
                        as its brothers or cousins?

That's it!

Food names are like
        family names

                with individual pieces
                        being related to each other

and thus,
        that explains why

                no two pieces
                of whatever

                        ever
                        do taste

the same—
no,
not ever!

Like:

toast
cheddar cheese
green beans
potatoes
milk
tomatoes
chicken
oranges
oatmeal
bananas
cucumbers
lettuce
and
watermelon
etc.
etc.

etc.

except
highly refined

processed
packaged food

(sometimes preferable)

because
she can always know

what she's getting
ahead of time

because
you see—

junk food
is cloned

no cousins or brothers!

FOOD FEELINGS

Often she hears people
    commenting on

       the taste of their food,

  but she hasn't yet heard anyone
     say anything about

       how it FEELS!

To her
    what's quite obvious

      (sometimes even more than the taste)

     is what it FEELS like
      in at least

        three places

Over her tongue,
   down her throat and on

      the inside side of her cheeks

   each bite of food
     is FELT

    very differently.

Sometimes it is
    interesting to notice

       this difference

    but other times it makes
      eating too intense

      an experience!

GETTING SQUISHED

Something she's never told anyone
      because it seems so odd
            and because
                  she's never heard anyone else
                    talk of it
                        and yet
                              for her it has always been
                                quite obvious …

                              Ever since she's been a girl
                  she would dream up
              elaborate plans
      (she called them "games" when she was little)
      that would always end up
with her getting squished.

That's enough about this
      for right now
            because writing this down
                is causing
                    her insides
                        to come out.

                It's uncomfortable
            when this happens
         and she doesn't quite know
what to do
      when all of a sudden
            it seems
                that her skin
                    is only for looks.

                          It's as if her skin quits
                    doing its job
              of keeping what's on the inside
           side of her skin in
         and keeping the world on the
      outside side
of her skin.

All in all
      when this happens

she can still see her skin,
      but it starts losing its feel
          as if it's not there
             being that   line-drawn-in-the-sand
               that it's supposed to be
                    the demarcation between
                    all of what's her
                      and all
                 of everything
               else outside of her being.

             Her insides leak out
and world outsides seep in.

She becomes very hyper-vigilant
      trying desperately to keep
          her insides and
             all the world outsides
          sorted into their proper places
        even though her skin
     has stopped working
the way it is meant to.

She becomes very scared
      and sometimes looks
          like she's acting crazy
             when all she is trying to do
               is keep insides and outsides
              sorted out
                 so she can
              remain only one person
        in all of the outside world.

          One time when a teenager
        she heard a hospital worker proclaim
      that all that was needed was to
whip her back into shape again.

Instantly, she knew
      that she knew
          that she knew
             (and she still knows it now)
               that what she really needed was to
                  be squished back into shape
                    to be tightly squished

so she could feel
where the end of her was
and feel
the physical sensation that
all of that which
belonged there
was   there
on the inside side
of where her skin was.

And she needed to stay squished up
for long enough
to relax into
whatever it was
that was now substituting
for the feel of her skin
because only then
could her body feel safe—
all put
back together
with all her insides
feeling in place
in their own space
on the inside side
of where her skin was.

And then   a little while later
she could feel where her own body
was located and   then could
physically sense
the world outside of her skin
was truly not oozing into her,
but was back in its
rightful place
in its own space
on the outside side
of where her skin was.

To get the feel
of her own skin back
she would very

very

very

very

very

s l o w l y

take off or   take away
whatever   it   was
that was
acting as the substitute
for her own skin
because if
this happened
slow enough
without
a big pressure difference
felt all at once
she could then resume
feeling her skin
which caused
her to know
just what was where
and on which side
of her skin
it resided.

… and then
the upset
was over.

MY SCHOOL DAYS HAZE

STARTING THIRD GRADE

Too much new
    for back-to-school
        is why I just   don't like it,

    though
        each new thing
           all by   itself

           is entirely
             acceptable.

New shiny shoes
    I do so love
        new ribbons in   my hair

    a freshly pressed
        brand new pink   dress
        Oh   …

           ain't I
             debonair!

My satchel packed
    with all new things
        with all the stuff I   need

    sits on the floor
        next to the   door
          just waiting

           for me
             to leave!

New class lists
    posted on the   doors;
        the students find their   names.

    They take their   seats
        and wait to   see
          what will
           this brand new teacher
             say!

"Unpack supplies.
    Get settled in.
        My name is on the   board."

  On and on
      her voice keeps   speaking
         way much

             too many
               words.

Her voice   plows on
   it will not   quit.
    Words heap up in a   pile,

    while yellow   chalk
       adds   to the   talk.
       School

         just ain't
           my   style.

Time for   recess.
   Go   outside.
    New   playground has no   shade.

    Kids   race about;
      they run and   shout.
      At   recess

        I might
          die.

I stand   real still
  and close   my   eyes.
    The   teacher comes   by   me.

    She does   smell   nice,
     but I've   made up   my mind …
     I right now

       quit
        third grade.

PHENOMENA IN ORBIT

feelings are difficult   to know   and to understand
    but that is just   the nucleus
      around which
       all the resulting phenomena   orbit

PHENOMENA ONE

take   for instance
     the attributing of feelings   to   inanimate objects

       like   the lonely glove
        who lost   its mate
     or   the happy juice pitcher
        who just got filled up   with orange juice   now in it

and because   inanimate objects   can have feelings of their own
    the objects themselves   become   "people-ified"
      so it's easy   to have

       gloves who …   or
       juice pitchers who …
        etc.,   etc.,   etc.

and from there   it's only one   logical step
    to strike up   a   relationship   with
      friendly   inanimate objects

    who   most of the time   make
      the very best   kind   of friend
   she could   ever hope   to have

      always   the same
     never changing   predictable friends
       she can count on

and following this logic   forty years later   she now understands
   why   the little girl   so desperately wanted
     to take her friends—

      the   lonely glove   and
      the   happy juice pitcher—

along with her   to school
on that winter day
so long ago

feelings are difficult   to know   and to understand
but that is just   the nucleus
around which
all the resulting phenomena   orbit

PHENOMENA TWO

take   for instance
the relating of   the essence of human beings   to objects

like   wanting to be a rubber band
when she grew up
or   thinking her sister
was a bike

because to her   this was   the only way   she had
to express   the ideas   inside her head

and since   people around her
didn't like   listening
to talk   like this

she learned quickly   not to say the words aloud
but   to only say them   quietly   inside of herself

and this is the rule   she made to follow:

Don't say words together
that   make people   be things
or   make things   be people.

in fact   it was one   of the rules
she had made   for herself   to follow—

one that belonged
to the set   of rules called

HOW TO BE A NON-ALIEN

now   forty years later   she can understand

what words to say   instead of

"I want to be   a rubber band."
             or
"My sister is   a bike."

rubber bands   squeezed things   together   and held them
        tightly in place   forever

            rubber bands were   so admired
                that she aspired
                    to be one

        for she couldn't imagine anything better
                than to grow up   to be

                    something   that could help
        to put back together again

                the pieces   of people
                        whose insides   had   come apart

today   she is in   a helping profession
        but   way back then

            she didn't have   all these words
        at her command
                to explain it

                she only knew   that
        she wanted to be   a rubber band

                even though   she also knew
                    not to   say it

feelings are difficult   to know   and to understand
        but that is just   the nucleus
                around which
                all the resulting phenomena   orbit

PHENOMENA THREE

        take   for instance
                her incongruent responses   to events

that evoke
feelings in   others

like   laughing   when
her grandpa   died
or   clapping for
an ambulance   going by

(because   as a little girl
she hadn't   yet developed
PHENOMENA   FOUR)

because   as a little girl   whenever
she hears about   or sees   an event

the first things   that come   to her mind
are the   very immediate facts
of some   isolated part

of the   whole picture
pertaining   to the matter

like   when she heard   her grandpa died
the first   picture that popped into her mind

was of Bozo   the clown
with his   hair dyed   orange

and it made her   laugh
because   Bozo's orange hair
looks funny

and   she hated   loud sounds
and had learned   from watching   at the parade

that   when loud noises come   and people clap
the loud noises   will stop or go away

so   a few days later
when a loud   ambulance siren
was on the street   by her school

she clapped   in order to   make it stop
and it did   even though
she had to clap a long time

43

until the nun   jerked her arm   and said
she was   a bad girl   to clap

and then she   talked back   (to explain)
and had to stand   in the corner
for the rest of   the morning

the nun told her   she needed to learn   to be quiet
and not to   talk back   when being scolded

and that   all that little girls   needed to do
was to say   "yes ma'am"   and smile
whenever   an adult   spoke to them

so she tried it   and found
it worked well   except for the times
when "yes ma'am" was   the wrong answer

so   she left off the   "yes ma'am"   and just smiled
whenever people   talked to her

which really did work
much better   for living

in the   world-people   world
with grown-ups in it

feelings are difficult   to know   and to understand
but that is just   the nucleus
around which
all the resulting phenomena   orbit

PHENOMENA FOUR
take   for instance
her lack of response to
the expressed feelings   of others

like   standing there   silently
after someone   gives her a compliment
or   simply looking   at a person
who has told her about some   tragic event

because   even today   forty years later

sometimes   when someone else   displays
     an emotion or feeling   of any kind

it takes   a very long time
     for her   to process

so long   in fact   that most of the time
     the other person
walks away   before
she ever has a chance

     to think of something
     to say   back to them   in response

     and she knows   when this happens
that other people   think she is rude

     or that she   just doesn't care
     about what   they have said

it makes her   really sad   whenever this happens
     and she can understand why   people often think
     she doesn't   care about them

which really   isn't at all true
     because she really   does care

     and often cries and prays for them
once the   feelings catch up

     usually when she   is back home
     privately alone   in her room

she   wishes that people   could look inside her
and see how   her insides work
     so they could   come to know

that it   takes her   so much longer   than most
     to get   from the words   of others
     to feelings   of her own

     and then   to translate her   own feelings
     back into words   that show
     that she understands and cares …

feelings are difficult   to know   and to understand
    but that is just   the nucleus
        around which
           all the resulting phenomena   orbit

and the   PHENOMENA   goes on
    and on
        and on

forever affecting
    all of her life
        spreading
           from the nucleus
              outward
                like   the ripple of rings
                  that never stop
              growing larger
           and larger

      in circles   around
        where the stone
          hits the water

          until the life
            of the stone
              is over

FEELINGS difficult to know and understand — PHENOMENA ONE — ATTRIBUTION OF FEELINGS TO THE EVENTS THAT EVOKE THEM — PHENOMENA TWO — OF RESPONSE — PHENOMENA THREE — INCONGRUENT RESPONSES TO THE EXPRESSING OF THE ESSENCE OF FEELINGS IN OTHERS — PHENOMENA FOUR — OBJECTS — LACK OR FEELINGS OF OTHERS TO INANIMATE OBJECTS — nucleus

GETTING OUT OF TOWN

when the info she needs   is somewhere   inside her
          and   she just   can't   find it
                    right then   when   she needs it

          she calls this   ultimate inside frustration

                    and when she   was   a girl
                    she coped   by showing an array   of behaviors

                    that world-people outside of her   labeled
                              "inappropriate"

she learned   over time   that   silence   was more acceptable
          to the people   in the world   outside her
                    so   she tried   it

          and this   is   what she did:

                    she made   a map with   a city   in the middle
                              named   Ultimate Inside Frustration

                    and then   she drew   a road   to take
                              to get herself   out   of this town

after that   whenever   she found
          that she was in town
                    she knew exactly   what to do

          instead of   staying in town
                    she would   turn and   run down

                              the road   with the   sign
                    pointing   "OUT"

this meant that   what people   outside of her   saw
          was that rather than
                    hitting or hurting   herself

          she would   just sit in her seat

and   be silent
in the beginning   outside people   didn't act
badly   towards her   whenever she
followed   her map

and took   the Silent Road   out
of the town   called
Ultimate Inside Frustration

but about the time   she perfected   this strategy
and became   an expert   at following   her map

(so good   in fact
that she now found
it much preferable
to just live
on Silent Road
by ignoring the world
around her
never anymore
ever having to go
into the town
of Ultimate Inside Frustration)

and it was   around this time   that
the people outside her   decided

that now they   didn't like   her new way   of acting
because now,   they said,   she was   being too quiet

so they took her away   to live at   a place   far away
from everything   she knew   and was comfortable   with

but it didn't   matter   to her
as   she had   already decided
to live on   Silent Road

as far away   on the map   as possible
from   the city of
Ultimate Inside Frustration

and this is where   she lived   at 1025 Silent Road

for the next   several months   of her life

      all the time watching   in the world   outside her
gathering up all   the info   she needed
    and then could use

        to draw   more roads
on the map   inside her

        so that   after a   l   o   n   g   time
     her map   had more than   one way

        to leave   the town of
        Ultimate Inside Frustration

during those months   she drew   and erased
     and reconstructed   her   inside map
     using all the info   she saw   outside her

   watching   very carefully
     so she always   would know when

        she was   heading towards   that town
    she didn't want   to ever be in

that way   she could choose
     one of her   very own roads   to travel
       from the map   she had drawn   inside her

   heading   away from   that horrible town
     she never again
        wanted to   be in

        that town   of
        Ultimate Inside Frustration

just in case   there are others   who may   want to draw
     their own map   inside them

       she thought it might be helpful if
she wrote down   the names   of the roads

she found   that were   sometimes helpful
      to take   to get   out of town

whenever she found
     herself   on her way
       to that   place of

    Ultimate Inside Frustration
and she had to   pick quick
    which   road to take

    because   if she would wait
'til   she found herself in the middle of town

    it would be   too late

    becoming impossible   to take
any of   the roads   leading out

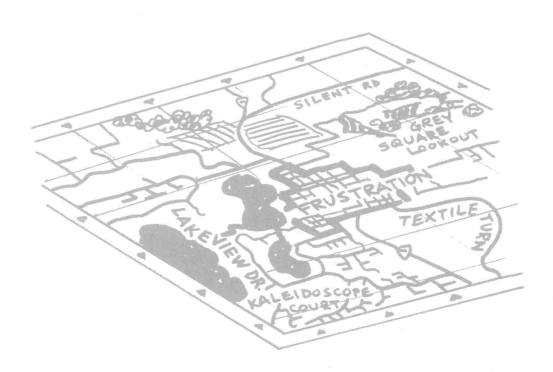

names of the roads on the map

leading out of

the town of

Ultimate Inside Frustration

Silent Road   where she can disengage from the outside world

Kaleidoscope Court   where she can find comfortable-looking matching colors to see

Gray Square Look Out   where she can see the repeating pattern of the same speckled

                           gray squares on the floors everywhere

Hummingbird Lane   where she can silently hum the same few measures of the very same

                           tune over and over and over again

Lake View Drive   where she can watch or listen to moving water in the lake

                           or in the shower or in the sink or the toilet

Textile Turn   where she can stroke something very smooth and soft or

                           something with a repetitive pattern of texture

WRITING SCRIPTS AHEAD OF TIME

when new situations   arise in her life
     often   she is silent
       and without reaction
     simply because   there is   no reaction inside her

a long time ago   she figured out
     that it's really not   a good idea
       to be like   a magician   pulling a rabbit   out of a hat

and just   pull out   any old   behavior
     already inside her   and apply it
       to something new   that's happening today

       because   whenever she used that magician strategy
       it never worked   very well—

         she always got   some strange animal
       never the   expected rabbit—

         which then   caused people
           to act strangely   towards her,
       to call her   crazy   or
         to just not like her

from watching   all the world-people   all around her
     she discovered

       that   all sorts of behaviors
     even the   new ones   they had never yet tried

       somehow
        had already
       been placed
        inside **them**

after watching   for a long time
     she finally   decided
       that   all of   the world-people
     must have been   made this way
       from   the very beginning

                    even   before
            they were   born

she   didn't know why   she was made   different

        but   even if she   did know
               it   wouldn't really   much matter

        as right then
               she just needed   to figure out   a way
                       to get   new behaviors
               put   inside her

                       before the   time came
                       to search   through all of her
               "how-to-react-behavior-data"

                           in tomorrow's future
                                when she   would need
                           to   find it

in order   for her   to act   in a new way
        the   behavior desired

               must have   somehow
been previously   placed
        inside her

               the idea   being   quite simple:

in order to   retrieve the data
               it must first   be entered

next   she had to   figure out
        how to   enter the data

               without   ever knowing
        what the data   might be

               in order   to discover

                       what the   data that was missing
               inside her   might be

                       she   watched all the   world-people
                              outside her   to see

how they behaved
when they   were together—

what   they said
and how   they acted
towards   each other

then   whenever   she liked   what she saw
she made   a story

always   in the same order

like this:

1.   situation …

2.   what to say …

3.   how to act …

and when   the story   was finished
she put her name   in it

and   that is how   she entered
unknown data   inside her

ahead of the time   when she   might someday need it …

before that   tomorrow-time came   to search   through all of
her   "how-to-react-behavior-data"

that had already   been previously
placed and stored   inside her—

by writing   the scripts   ahead of   the time
she would   act them out

just in case   she would
one day   need them

**HOW TO BE A NON-ALIEN
(RULES ABOUT SPEAKING)**

the realities   of her existence
        on this   world-people planet

                tend to   magnify   her differences
                        every day
                in numerous ways

                        while   she tries   to minimize
                                the impact   her differences
                                        will have   upon others

                        because   life is easier
                                for all of them   and   for her
                                        when   she doesn't   appear

                                to be   an alien
                                        living in   human skin
                                                roaming   around on the earth

she has a   set of rules
        engineered   specifically   to cause
                her to   look   as if   she belongs

                        in   this world-people planet
                that others   call home

                        but   to her   feels more
                                like   a place   she is visiting

                        while   biding   her time
                                until she can go   wherever the   place is
                                        where   she might   belong

until then   she lives by   the rules   she created
        designed especially   with world-people in mind

                people who think   themselves to   be tolerant
                        patient   and kind

                but   nevertheless still
                        have their   own limits

                    on   just how much   difference
they   can handle

        at any   particular time
                during the day   or night

                    how to be a non-alien
                    (a partial listing of the rules
                    from the chapter on speaking)

1.   Use words   that could make   a blind man see
                the picture   in her head

                        without using any more words
                than absolutely   needed

                        and   setting a limit
                of two minutes   a picture   in which
                        to say them.

2.   Put words   in three groups   to describe
                the three   most important parts
                of her picture.

                (When she got older
                        she discovered
                that each   group of words
                        was called   a sentence!)

3.   Remember to stop   and take   a breath
                between each group   of words

                            because   three groups
                said   all together
                without any breaks

                    cause   world-people   to frown
                        and   then not listen.

4.   Besides taking   a breath
                she found   that world-people
                        listen   much better

                    if each   group of words
                        has   a beginning

and an end to
the sound of them.

5. Another thing she discovered
was the world-people order
of topic importance

like this:

#1 people
#2 feelings
#3 things

and in addition to their order

they want the talking words of others
to match their world-people word arithmetic

like this:

People can equal Feelings.
People cannot equal Things.

Using world-people word arithmetic
an example of how they want words
to be said would be like this:

It's O.K. to say, "Mom is mad."
but it's not O.K. to say, "Mom is a volcano."

so for her to look as if she is
someone who just might fit in the world-people world

where she doesn't belong

she must use real words for speaking
and put them in world-people form

with these five rules
being among the most important ones

for her to follow

in order to not be an alien on earth
who gets in trouble

GIFTS FROM MY STUDENTS

WHEN BEST FRIENDS ARE THE CEILING TILES

her best friends are the ceiling tiles

no matter what happens during the day
or how she feels   inside her

she knows these friends are always there   for her
whenever she   might need them

no one could ever ask   for friends   more loyal or   more true

friends to stick with her   through thick and thin
for better or   for worse

no matter what   she knows she's got
good friends   in ceiling tiles

when things   outside her become   a bit too much
and keeping them   sorted out becomes   a stressor

she knows she can always   relieve the pressure

by seeking out her friends

hanging out with them   even for   a little while
she can feel restored and   back in balance

thanks to her friends   the ceiling tiles

she doesn't tell other people about   her friends   the ceiling tiles
knowing they just wouldn't   understand it

and to her   it is not important to have
another person "get it"

but things have changed since yesterday
when she met a boy named Francis

who also takes   great comfort in
gazing at ceiling tiles

Francis, being the boy that he is,   hasn't yet lived

in the world   long enough
          to become comfortable with   his differences

and people outside   of him   have let him know
          they think he   is   quite "different"

so when Francis needs to   soothe himself
          by gazing at   ceiling tiles

          he lays on the floor   and says, "I am weird."

but he knows that he needs to   look up at his friends
          to see all of   their cool patterns

          of hundreds of dots   all looking the same
          in each and every square

she knows that   **Francis is *very* smart**
          because he knows   just what he   needs to do
          to take good care of himself

he knows when   he needs   to take a break
          to look at   the ceiling tiles

          the only problem   with this
          is that people might   think he is weird   when he isn't

          it's just that in some   particular ways
               Francis is just plain different

the name of this difference is called autism

          which is a normal way   of thinking and being
          for a very small group   of people

but because this group of people   is small

          all the other people   notice and call
          their different ways   a "difference"

when a person   like Francis   has autism
          it is normal for them   to have   non-people friends

          and often they like   to look at things
               such as ceiling tiles

to see lots of dots   in really cool patterns

     with all of the dots   in each square
        always   looking   exactly the same
          as all of   the others

     this predictable   repeating pattern   of sameness
        tends to be   comforting
     (more comforting than the comfort that people can give)

     and can restore
(in a person with autism)

     an upset inside balance

when   **Francis is being smart**   to take care of himself
     by looking at ceiling tiles

     the kids at school say to him,
"You're so weird."   because
     this is what they see:

        all of a sudden   Francis jumps up from his seat
   and flops down   on the floor

        it disturbs the class
and some kids laugh

       and say, "Francis, you're so weird."

and nobody knows   **how smart Francis is being**

    to take care of himself   by looking up
      at the ceiling tiles

because nobody can see
     Francis' smart part
     with their eyes

     the only thing   kids' eyes can see

       is Francis jumping up   from his seat
        and flopping down   on the floor

maybe Francis could change   what the   other kids see
   so they could   never-in-a-million-years guess

when he was taking a break
to look up and gaze   at his friends   the ceiling tiles

like maybe instead of   moving all of his body

Francis could stay in his seat
and just move his eyes
to look up   at the ceiling tiles

then, if any of the kids   happened to look at him

all they would see
would be

Francis sitting still in his seat

the very same way   exactly just like
all the rest of the kids   in the room

and nobody would have
any reason just then

to get any idea in their brain

to act mean or   to call Francis names

JUST FOLLOW THE RULES, STUPID

When reading a book
    you start in the front
        on page 1
    and proceeding in numerical order

        page after
            numbered page,

        exactly
            in their 1, 2, 3
                numbered order,

        you keep reading
            until

            you reach
          the very last
           of all
              of the words

           and find
             that the only thing
                left to see
            is some
              white pages
                and then

            the book's
             inside
                back cover …

That's when
    you can know

        that the story
    you're reading

        has come
            to its very own end

        and then,
            and only then,

might you conclude

that the book
you've been reading
is done being read

so therefore
this book

can be put
back on the shelf

or exchanged
for another.

So, why is it
that reading
never works for me

when always
I follow
the rules?

every day,
every time,

when my work is all done

I open my book
to the
same page 1 …

I sit quietly
in my seat
so as not to disturb

all the rest
of the students
who are finishing their work …

Then, when the time is up

I put my book
in my backpack until
the next time comes

when my work
    is all done

and I
    must sit
        quietly still …

    then, once again
        I pull out my book
           and follow the rules …

    I start on page 1
        as I know I should

           over and
        over and
           over again

             every time …

But I don't
    understand

    why reading
a book
    never works
        as it should

    when I'm careful
        to follow
           the rules …

    never do I get
        to the end
           of my book …

    It must be
        because
           I'm stupid.

ARBITRARINESS

If   an orange
     is   an orange
         is   an orange
            is an orange

        then   why isn't
           a banana   a yellow

               a grape   a green

              and
                 an apple   a red

                   instead of

                     the arbitrary names

                       assigned
                         to
                           them?

TAKE WHAT?

"Take care," my teacher
          says to me

                    each time
                    I leave
                              her room.

I'd do
          what she wants
                    if only
                    I knew

                              WHICH

                    of all of
                              the things
                                        on her desk

                    the name
                              of "Care"
                                        goes to.

Each day I watch
          her eyes to see
                    if I can tell

                    just where
                    they might come to look,

                              HOPING that
                                        she'll look at "Care"

                                        so I might
                                                  get a clue

                    of just
                              which item
                              she wants
                                        me to take

                    every day
                              when
                                        I leave
                                                  her room.

LUCKY STARS

How can you count
    your lucky stars

        when
    you own no stars at all?

And if,
    perchance

        you did
    own some …

        how would you
        come to know

          which stars were lucky

          and

          which stars weren't?

HELPING HATE DISSIPATE

my student wanted to know
    why all the kids
        were hating him

          including the kids
      he didn't even know

he felt so bad
    his head hung low

      initially his question
        an indiscernible mutter

          but the third time around
      was spoken more boldly

    it took four days
to figure out
    what he meant
      when he said

      that
    all of the kids
were hating him

when we walked in the halls
    between class

      where students scurry
    like ants

        who can't wait
          for a picnic

          my student sometimes
            walked against

        the flow of foot traffic

    which caused him

      to get bumped
and jostled

more often than not

after confirming
that my student equated

being bumped
in the halls

with kids hating him

I was able
to explain
to him

the unwritten rule
that world-people know

about

which side
of the hall
to walk on

with his
newfound knowledge

of hallway
traffic patterns

along with reviewing
his own
spatial relationship

to all
of that movement

my student
now bustles
contentedly along
with all
of the other
hallway ants

on their way
to their
various picnics

PLANET GO THERE

CAR OF WAIT

INTRODUCTION

All of her life
        right up to the present

                she's made   each day work
                using her inside system

                        that took years of watching

                        both inside
                                and outside of her skin

        to decipher
                just what works how

                in each separate place
                        and then to continuously   meld together

                        from the two separate   planets
                                divided by   skin

        a workable understanding of   how to live out

                the life God gave her
                plunked right down   in the middle of

                        a world full of people

                        where she feels like
                                an alien.

So
        she wrote this story

                about   how things work

                and a synopsis
                        in a nutshell
                        goes
                                like this:

Autism lives
        in the   Place of Here.

Transition continually
demands of Autism,   "Go There."

        every day
        Autism has

                such a   hard time

figuring things   out

because
        you see

        it is
                very difficult

        to get

        to Planet Go There
                in her Car of Wait …

Now
        if you want
                a more filled in   picture

                keep reading   the words
                        of this   unfolding story

                        so that   you might
                                come to   appreciate

                the explosions
                of children   and

                        their parents'
                                worries.

THE PLACE OF HERE

Autism lives in
      the Place of Here
              which is   an actual   physical space.

         When she was young
               the   Place of Here   was

           everything on   the inside side
              of her skin.

   Over the years
        she practiced   and fine-tuned

        her ability   to include
           the things   from There

           (way out   on the other side
             of her skin)

        as temporary parts
        of the   Place of Here

           as her perceived need
           for such   inclusion
              arose.

  And this is how   Autism grew up
      as an alien girl

        who had been
           plunked right   down

         in the middle of
           a world-people   world:

  She came to include
        in the   Place of Here

        those immediate things
           just outside   of her skin

        that she perceived
           pertained to her.

As she grew taller and wiser

    she came to know
    that it was better

       for her
       as an alien girl

         living in a   world-people world

    when   she could include
    in her   Place of Here

       more   rather than less

       of those things
         outside of   her skin

       (those things
       out there   in the
         world-people world).

So now   as a woman

    Autism's actual   physical space
       of the Place   of Here

      is sometimes   e x p a n d i n g and
       at other times   contracting

      depending upon

        her immediate
      in-the-now   perception

      of each   current   ·
        social situation

  so that   she sporadically adopts

    the things   from There
    to the   Place of Here

      trying to fit   herself

(even though   she knows
      she's an alien)

into   her place
in   the
      world-people   world.

As the   Place of Here
    e x p a n d s and   contracts

     with each
     social encounter
       presented   to her

      one thing remains
       for sure

and that   is that

     everything on
    the inside side
      of her skin

      always remains
       the constant core

      of the   Place of Here

     which in reality

       is physically
     contained in

     but never a part   of
       the world-people   world

     constantly causing
    her   to feel

      like an   alien

     roaming around
    on the face

      of   the earth.

PLANET GO THERE

Planet Go There
    is the physical space
        on the other side
        of the   Place of Here.

          In appearance
          if one could   actually see
            the two spaces

    they look to be
        neighboring properties
        with no space
          between them

          and literally speaking
            they actually are!

Often   trouble arises because
    these neighbors   don't understand
    each   the other.

        They have their   differences

        one of them   being   .
          in   how they travel.

People from There
    drive Cars of Go   and
        have a good sense
        of direction

          somehow   mysteriously knowing
          just how to   get There

          (or how to get   anywhere)

    simply by using
        their   world-people method
        of travel   that

          Autism calls their
          get-up-and-Go
            Cars.

Meanwhile   aliens who live

each in their   very own
            Place of Here

            always drive Wait Cars   which
                    simply aren't mobile

                    so can't   Go There
                        (or go anywhere   else)

until Autism has   everything
            thought out   ahead of time

            knowing   which turns
                    will be taken   and
                    just how to
                            take them

            knowing which
            stationary   scenery
                    will be
                    in its very
                            own space

            in the very   same place
            it has always been

                    on each   and every
                    previous trip
                            she has   taken.

Because of   the different kinds   of
            cars that they drive

                    by the time   that
                    Autism is actually   able
                            to get There

                    the world-people   have gone
                            in their   Cars of Go

            from There
            to There

to There
and then   to where
          only God knows!

(But they   themselves
     probably know   where,   too ...)

     a fact that
          further frustrates

          all the drivers   of all of
               the Cars of Wait

who have   already
     painfully compared
     and know

          that the
          Cars of Wait
               are always

          inferior   to

          the Cars of Go

               for the most part
     due   to their being

          greatly outnumbered   in
               the world-people   world.

CAR OF WAIT

TRANSITION

CAR OF WAIT

Oftentimes   one will find

    Autism sitting
        in her   Car of Wait

      spinning her wheels
        as she perseverates

          round   and round   and round
          she talks

going faster and faster
    in her Time of Stuck

    but no matter what

       it's very hard
       to get anywhere
         in a Car of Wait.

Most times   it is helpful
    if a person
      from There
      says, "STOP"

       in a way
       that   is both
         kind and   definite

    because each instance
      of perseveration
      needs to have limits

        so it doesn't take on
        a life of its own

         and burn out

      in which case

      it will   then have had
        no use.

Time-limited   instances
        of perseveration

        with no limits
                on the number
                of separate times
                        to do it

                is the   very best
                way to go
                        because

as Autism   talks and
        talks   and talks   some more

        with words always going
                to the same nowhere

                with limits in   place
                        so burnout   won't happen

the repeating words
        of perseveration

        serve to
                build
                a bridge
                        to Transition.

Sometimes it takes
        many instances   for Autism
                to perseverate   but

                gradually   over time
                        this activity serves

                        as a precursor for Autism
                                to take on Transition.

Sometimes   perseveration
        is Autism's way

        of getting ready   to accept

        Transitions, "GO"   so that

when all is said   again and
    again and   again
            over and   over

Autism might   laboriously

    pick up   her Car of Wait
    and carry it   carefully

        over the line

        and plunk it
            right down

        in the place
        of the space called

            Planet Go There.

But   until this time comes
    Transition and Autism are   archenemies

        an everyday battle
        waiting to be fought

            a lifelong war
            never able

            to be won.

    Transition says,   "GO!"
            and
    Autism says,   "NO!"

                the sides have been chosen
                their fight is on

    Transition demands,   "GO THERE!"
            while
    Autism insists,   "STAY HERE!"

            two wills collide
            dig in their heels

                and

the battle ensues

Transition commands,   "GO THERE NOW!"

Meanwhile

Autism has run out   of words
       but   nevertheless

fights to the end
with her behavior meltdown.

And even though   Autism
   fights with bravery

is loyal and true   even willing
to die for   her cause

she will never be given
a Medal   of Honor
for bravery or valor

but instead
for the rest of   her life

whenever
she gets   stuck

in the place of   Transition

Autism will become
a prisoner of war.

It might have been different
if in the beginning

Autism had had
the ability to   use

enough right words
to explain

her position   of
"I have to   stay
in the Place of Here

because Here is
all I can be
right at this   very
moment of upset

in this
snapshot
of time."

World-people may not
quite understand

that in   her Time of Stuck
Autism can't

imagine forward

being   quite literally
Stuck

in the facts   and emotions
of Here   like
a freeze-frame
in a movie

totally unable   to "GO"
anywhere.

Autism wishes
that world-people   could see

just how impossible
it is for her
to leave the   Place of Here

without being
devoured

by Chaos, Confusion and Conflict

when she
becomes
trapped

in the
Time of
Stuck.

It isn't   that
Autism   won't
"GO THERE!"   …

the reality   is
that she   can't.

EPILOGUE
(OR HINTS FOR THE HELPERS)

To facilitate
    Autism getting
        her Car of Wait

        over the border
          into the place

          of the space of
            Planet Go There

give her

        lots of permission
        to STOP
          when she's Stuck

        and   to WAIT
          'til she's   safe

which is contrary
    to the ways
    of the world

        but   if done
        consistently

          over and   over

will help
    Autism get   to
    Planet Go There

        and ultimately
        one day

          to take up   residence

        to live
        in her   place

          in your world.

SHADES OF LEMONADE

PAPER WORDS

Paper words
    can be heard;
        so speak up ink
           and say them!

        Speaking words
           are burdensome;
               they get her
                  lost   and tangled.

               So,   pen and ink
               are her first choice
                  to voice
                     what she's not saying.

When speaking   words
    two people should
        take their turns
           to say them.

        Start words   now
           then stop   and wait
              and listen   some:
                  adds up to conversation.

But,   starting words
    and   stopping them;
        then,   hearing words
              and   seeing faces

        is much   too much
           to keep track   of
              when having
                  conversation.

So,   paper words
    are much preferred.
        Speak up ink;
           now say them!

        Listen people
           to the ink;
              you won't get
                lost or   tangled!

AFTER RAIN SWING-RIDES

blue-sky
    hazy air
       after
          the storm
             has passed

swing seat

    colorless
       puddle rain

          soaking the seat
           of her pants

a rain pants
    trade-off

       so
          the alien girl
           might fly

swing chain's
    gray-purple squeaks

       streaking
         through
           time

white-blue
    strong air

       pressing
        her front
          and then   her back

          rhythmically

           over   and over
             again   and again

             as she pumps
              her swing into
                after-rain
                 places

pressure waves
    of blue-sky air

       rhythmically
         comfort her

            as she pumps
              higher
                higher

                 higher still

craving more

    and then
       still more

          of the   push-pull
            color-feel

             of white-blue sky
              against her

                she demanded
                  her orange-hot
                    needle-prick legs

                      to pump
                      still

                          higher

higher until …
    her body
       could touch
        and then
          become part of

          something
           bigger

            than
              all of
                her alien
                  being

thus …
    with gray-purple
      swing chains

        squeaking
          through time

           the alien girl
              became lost   to herself

                as she pumped
                 her swing

                   higher
                     and
                       higher …

white-blue
    sky waves

      pressing her   out of
        her alien being

          into sky wave
          color-oneness …

            for a moment

              transcending   all of
              her alien self

                in her swing seat

                  puddle-dark
                  pants

DOG WALK AIR COLORS

brown soft
> hush puppy skin folds
>> swaying to and fro

> as short legged
>> clippetty-clops
>>> echo off the sidewalk

the pink-yellow air
> of a going down sun
>> allows the girl

> and the dog
>> forward walking room
>>> into the future

>> by providing
>>> a reliable
>>>> unchanging pattern

>> of air color rhythm
>>> every night   after day

>>>> every day   after night

>>> predictably reliable
>>>> over and over
>>>>> again and again

the girl
> lent the air colors
>> a space inside her

> adopting
>> the yellow-pink air
>>> along with

>> its early-time night
>>> of lavender-blue
>>>> to herself

then …
      tying the dog
          by his house

she went
      back inside of
          her alien self

      to hide
          from
              a world

        she didn't belong to
        and
            was not a part of

         but one from which
           she could
              see and borrow

         dog walk
           air colors
              from

         to become

             for a moment
                something bigger

           than
              the alien girl
                she was

A STORY FOR FLORICA
ABOUT
MAKING AN ALIEN CRY

There is an alien who
      for more than 49 years
            has roamed the earth

                never being able to become
                    a full-fledged citizen

               because there has never been

                a way that has worked
               for the alien to get changed
                  into an acceptable creature

               who might be allowed
                    inclusion in a world-people world.

One day this alien
      saw a book with a name
            that included
               some of her favorite words

                  like rainbow and color

               so she ordered it
                  from Jessica Kingsley Publishers.

               When this book came
                  in the mail

               the alien was
                  so pleased to discover

               that the cover
                  was made
             in her favorite
                  blue color.

For the first several days
      she would pick up the book

just to hold it
and to look at it
and to see

if it were true
that the looks
of the cover

with its
color of blue

and pictures
of a rainbow
and a candle

still matched
her alien soul.

After some days
the alien did come to read
all of the words
on the cover

instead of only her favorite ones.

And as the alien
began to read

the words
on the inside pages

of this book
called

Autism—The Eighth Color of the Rainbow

she kept bumping into
her alien self

in the words
on the pages

BUT …

not as a dread disease,
an unsolvable problem,

a hopeless disgrace
or an unfixable misfit

not as an animal
who needed to be trained
with a cattle prod
to modify her behavior

not as someone to be electrocuted
with electric shock therapy
and then brought back to life
when she died

BUT,   instead of all this
(along with
even more stories
of treatment horrors)

the alien discovered
for the very first time
in her whole alien life

that somebody else
made a change

to make the world bigger

by imagining
an 8-hued rainbow

that she
could fit
her alien self into

as if
she was meant
to maybe
belong there

in the
world-people world

with all of the
world-people in it.

So   after some days
        of watching these rainbow colors

                and reading
                        again and again

                        the words
                        that created them

                        the alien decided

                to step into
                        that place
                in this rainbow

                        that seemed to be
                a place that
                        was waiting for her.

It was a very hard thing
        for the alien to do—

                after a lifetime of knowing

                        that she was utterly unacceptable—

                        to now change
                her thinking

                        and to take
                the first step towards

                        the place in the rainbow

                that Florica had made
                        for her.

It took a few tries
        but finally she did it

                by making an e-mail

                        and then soon after
                        by sending
                Paper Words

along with
a few more words

in a note
as a way
to say thank you

to the author
named Florica

for making
an 8-hued rainbow

that included
all of the people

both alien
and otherwise

who live in
this world.
Then
after a very short time

the e-mail was answered
with understanding and care

that made happiness to be
in the alien's heart

and also

for some unknown reason
to her

this understanding and care
made the alien cry

almost as if

she were maybe
part human

on the day
that her e-mail
was answered.

AN ALIEN NO MORE

I used to be an alien,
    but now I am no more.

        All because my thinking changed
           after meeting Florica.

Long ago I read a book, you see,
    when I was just a teen

        that told about an alien girl
           who was exactly just like me.

This book explained her human looks
    and how she spoke with words,

        but never, ever did she belong
           with humans in the world.

She lived inside a big building
    that looked very beautiful.

        And all the others who lived there
           were aliens just like her.

At the time I read this book I was confined
    for more than one whole year

        to a hospital run by the state
           that was called a mental institution.

This book gave me the hope
    that I might one day leave,

        to take my place with the aliens
           who were just like me.

Excitedly, I showed this book to a friend—
    a girl who was older and lived on my ward.

        She shook her head, warned me and said,
           "If you talk about this you will never be discharged."

So never from that day forth did I ever utter one single word
                about this book that I read   and the fact that I learned

                                that I was a real alien
                                        who lived on a world-people planet.

I was so relieved to learn of my alien status!
                It allowed me to figure out rules to the game

                                of how to act human in a world-people place
                                        while remaining the alien who was the real me.

Sometimes I did better;
                other times I did worse

                                at playing this game
                                        as my life ran its course.

For the past few years
                I've been writing (not speaking)

                                words about what it was like
                                        growing up as an alien

and then how it is now
                to be living an alien's life

                                as a grown-up adult
                                        in a world-people world.

My words made poems
                and my poems found a friend

                                who clearly didn't like me
                                        to use the word alien.

She was patient and kind
                and loved me to bits

                                and never once thought
                                        I was a stupid dimwit.

I came to trust her
                and then love her back

and one day became brave enough
to tell her the facts

about the book I had read
35 years ago that caused me to know

that I am a real alien
who lives on the earth.

This was the very first time
that I shared

the facts of my alien status
with any adult.

And now I have come to find out
that I'm not a true alien

and that my feelings of alien
are equal to the facts of autism!

(Also, it is interesting to note
that I really did know the difference

between books of fact
and those of fiction,

but had never linked
the two separate bits,

one with the other,
in a way

that would cause
me to know

that the book about aliens
was simply not true.)

THE RETURN OF THREE GREENS

(first green)

today-time is fading
  as the sun dips down
    below the horizon

  gently pulsating forth
    its blanket of green,
      getting forest-air ready for sleep

   quietness rolling in
    on the gentle waves
      of forest-calm soothing green

    as all creatures
     calm themselves
      into day's-end sleep

     while the leftover
     sun haze
      from air-today

      kisses
       the forest
        goodnight …

     its kiss of love
      a shimmering glow,
       lending shine to the forest-calm green …

     creating the green-sleep
      sound of night
       that relaxes away day-busies

      by its steady-beat rocking
       of green-wave low pitch
        blanketing the forest for night

(second green)

pastel green
 moving and floating
  yet going nowhere

 always within
  my reach

 fresh after-bath smell
  of a delicate
   clean-green newness

  each day
   of my being …

  … this start-over clean
   kind of green—
    elusive

   yet close
    to my reach

(third green)

bright-sunny-
 today's-here-
  let's-celebrate-green

 a bright-happy,
  steady-moving
   gurgling green

    its skip-happy
     easy-warm
      laughter to see

  sounding
   just like
    the very place

     where Big-Stone
      divides Water-Moving
     to make

the bubbling-drop
sound
of

green-yellow happiness
pleasantly dance
in my ears

MY FRIEND NAN

sparkling butter

    is my friend Nan

        that's how I perceive her

    sparkles sprinkling

        from her words

            as pleasantly I watch them

        drift from her

            into the air

                and into the world around them

            while her yellow glow

                that's butter soft

                    kindly brushes

                strokes of Air Word-Sparkle's

                shades of love

                    softly on my soul

LET'S DANCE ON THE BEACH!

Don't be sad for me

    when I am so happy

      that my words

  can show to you

      what my insides feel.

Let's dance on the beach

    'til the sun goes down

      because I can now

  show you words

      to match who I am!

Let's not be so fussy about

    what the words show,

      but let's skip pebbles

  across the waves

    in gladness

      that we can share

        with each other

  our souls!

AWAITING NEW-TODAY

sparkles sprinkling

    in the bed

started new-Day's picture

    in her head

       hinting colors

          of new-Day wonders

       not yet unfurled

          for nesting girls

          snuggled safely

             in a pocket

          tucked inside their movie-gray …

           five nesting girls awaiting

           new-Today

BREATHING DEEPLY

soft breezes
    on this   sunny-clear day
        meet up with   my skin
            in their   green-sea
                gentle way

            as I sit
            on a chair
            in the shade

                watching

            thoughts of the   future
        and what   it might bring
    make   lake-soft   little laps
  advancing … … … … … … … … … receding
matching   the sound   of   the waves

            as I sit
            on a chair
            in the shade

                observing

            the rocking   thought-colors
        inside of   my brain
      cradling   the space   of
    pastel … … … … … … … … … … future-thoughts
nurturing them   into   tomorrow

            as I sit
            on a chair
            in the shade

                contemplating

            how this   space-black
        in my brain
      last week   got reclaimed
    when outside humanness … … … … … … snuggled my skin
making space   in my brain   for   tomorrow

while today

I sit
on a chair
in the shade

   deep-breathing

Judy Endow, MSW

Judy is the parent of a son on the spectrum. She has worked with him and with other students on the spectrum developing visual systems that help provide supportive and positive behavior management that can be utilized by the student, their parents, teachers and other support persons. Judy recently moved to Madison, Wisconsin where she joined a school consultation team to support families, school districts and other agencies through Imagine a Child's Capacity, a private service agency. In addition, she offers workshops and presentations on a variety of autism-related issues. A board member of the Autism Society of Greater Madison, Judy is on the spectrum herself and brings a great depth of understanding and compassion to all of the work she does.

Ben Averill

Ben is a self-styled eclectic. He loves to work with children and has coached and instructed gymnastics for many years. Currently he is building a learning center for the arts located in a 150-year-old schoolhouse. An avid gardener and cook, Ben's recent work has been in ceramics, slate and wood. He lives with his wife in Madison, Wisconsin.